GOING TO DARJEELING WITH MY FATHER

GOING TO DARJEELING WITH MY FATHER

Nabin K. Chhetri

THE **BLACK SPRING**
PRESS GROUP

First published in 2026
By Eyewear Publishing Limited
The Black Spring Press Group
London, United Kingdom

Typeset with graphic design by Edwin Smet

ISBN 978-1-915406-48-4

This is a new collection, however a smaller selection of earlier versions of some of the poems appeared in 2016 in an American collection from Red Mountain Press in a very limited edition.

BLACKSPRINGPRESSGROUP.COM

For my Father Amber Bahadur Chhetri

Nabin K. Chhetri, born in Nepal, is a poet and writer based in Scotland. He holds an M.St in Creative Writing from the University of Oxford and an M.Litt. in The Novel from the University of Aberdeen. His fiction and poetry have received international recognition. He is the director of Mist and Mountain (UK), a Creative platform.

TABLE OF CONTENTS

GOING HOME

When all the work and wait is done,
I long to go to my country.
In October, the mud on the paddy fields dries up,
the earth sends a fragrance
I knew as a child.
The village roads wait for people
from Kuwait, the UK, Australia, the US.
The hibiscus and marigold
scatter along the sideways.
The smell of clothes, freshly-stitched,
hangs in the air as children pass by.
The nights fill up with tinsel lights.
Buses go with people on the hoods, and goats.
The stench of diesel in the marketplace
reminds me I can't belong elsewhere.
The little happiness that arrives
when I enter that creaking wooden door.

PAPER BOAT

Finally, the boat is made
for my six-year-old son.
A white paper one.
A dot of red ink in the front
is the navigation light.

The sail has been attached to its deck
made of a matchstick and a blue ribbon.
The bathtub has been filled up.
It's a few inches deep as I put my fingers in.

My son stands there
as we launch the boat, into the tub.
It makes small movements on the skin of water
as I blow it with a mouthful of air.
I watch him, eyes affixed on the boat
his heart is filled with joy,
with the cargo of happiness
it has brought.

MEMORIES OF A FORGOTTEN COUNTRY

Kancha – in this black and white photograph, you are five.
Our sister clutches a bouquet of plastic flowers
that were once a shade of pink.
Our father is seated in a pair of blue Wranglers.
It's the beginning of the '80s,
he has started a boarding school in Bharatpur,
a new-sprung town on the forest's other side.
He buys a Chinese bicycle, a Phoenix brand,
installs a small seat for you.
The slim tyres kick off a cloud of dust
as they crackle along the gravelled road to school.
You thumb the bell all the way,
your face telescoped on its curved steel covering.
This photo is taken in Dashain,
the only time we get new clothes –
father picks them, mostly jeans, white shirts,
ordering the tailor to take our measurements.
We love the smell of the clothes,
take turns sniffing. He cycles us all the way home,
our minds lit with the scent.

BIRDS

In my garden the rhododendrons are wild this year.
Their pink flowers cover the treetops.
Early May, the sparrows make their homes
under its branches.

On an evening like this one
even after the last light of the day fades
I long to sit, long and late –
listen to the sparrows
and their newly hatched chicks.

I do not understand their language
but know that they have a lot to share.

And I like to think of the baby sparrows
who do not know that a few feet above their nest
a big sky awaits
nor do they know they have wings.

One day, I might as well be sitting
and without my knowing
their wings will lift them up
to the sky of their dreams.

MOTHER

This January, my mother will turn seventy-three.
I remember as a child –
whenever I crawled by her side
caught the crease of her sari and cried.
She lifted me on her arm and carried me to my room.
She covered me with a blanket as I pretended to sleep.

Though I was small, I was old enough to read her face
the clear lines of her skin, the hollow of her cheeks,
the little islands of her smiles.

Now I see her again, closer, after many years.
Her hair greyed, her bespectacled eyes.
I remember those days –
so much has changed since then
but what has not changed is her smile.

Even today when she smiles
the little folds, circles, and curves
on her face, gather in celebration.

MOON

It’s winter here in Scotland,
pitch black out in the woods,
inside my tent, the silence deepens.
Only the chirping of birds
reminds me that I’m camping.
And when I remember you,
I also remember the moon,
so let me put a moon for you,
just above these woods –
the River Isla now lit up
with its phosphorescence,
and if you observe, a rugged way
passes along the sandbank
where a pair of swans live.
Last year, they had cygnets
trailing the watercourse;
the mother, with her long neck
came so near, you almost touched.

APPLE PICKING IN SHIMLA

As August draws to a close,
thick clouds loom beyond the hills of Kufri.
In sunlit orchards near Theog,
the apples ripen on the branches.
Over days and nights, their skin
turns pink, red and yellow.
The first bite shoots a burst
of clear white water. Soon,
they will hang from the branches
like a perfect gift. The apple pickers
fill their baskets until late evening,
singing songs of longing.
On one such evening,
I listen to those apple pickers,
the smell of the orchard spreading
over the village, thinking of the first apple
that might appear on the branch,
innocent of the harvest it will bring.

HAPPINESS

We walked into Denburn Wood that autumn,
our feet stirring the leaves, dry and curled.
To the north, a highway quietly moved
along the rim of a rapeseed field.
A deer stepped across, then vanished into the undergrowth.
The wind carried the smell of damp grass.
You passed me popcorn
and a flask of coffee.

Later, when we returned,
a wonderful evening, you said.
A ray of vermillion light lingered on your face
long after the trees had darkened.

That night when I went to bed after a cup of warm water,
I thought about how relentlessly we search for happiness.

Years after, you are gone.
As I lay bedridden inside the room,
it's autumn again.
The cherry blossoms shine on the pavement.
Damp but briefly lit by the late sun.

I remember that day –
your blue coat, the scent of coffee,
the sound of our steps in the leaves –
a quiet glow returns to my face
and with it, peace
though it's not the same evening,
not the same year.

THE GARDEN IN WINTER

I am talking about my garden
where my wife has planted dahlia, gerbera,
tulips, marigold, geranium and roses.
While we warm ourselves in the house,
the flowers brave the North Sea storm.
As it thrashes and beats upon their stems,
some bend and die at night,
while others refuse to give up.
When the sun brightens the yard,
they stand there, dressed obediently
in their colours. Look closely:
their bruised petals, broken branches,
their droopy stems – you will see
an angry note winter left in my garden.

LOCH MUICK CAMPING

It's May, and I am camping by Loch Muick.
A cool breeze stirs the fabric of my tent.
Nearby a river meanders downhill
towards the vast expanse of the Glen.
Hundreds of deer forage in the distance.
I boil the tea on the butane stove.
Its buzzing mingles with the sound of the river.

I open the tent flap and move the chair outside
watching the last light brighten the hills
between me and the nightfall.

GOING TO DARJEELING WITH MY FATHER

On the bus ride uphill, I sat beside you.
I must have been nine, then.

I would sit by the window
watching the landscape shift
on the tinted glass pane.

At Kurseong, the bus would stop
the old train station would pull up, staggering
through a haze of mist
the smell of burnt coal warming my nostrils.

You always got off the bus to buy something.
My eyes would follow you through the crowd
and as soon as you disappeared, my heart would skip a beat.
Life returned when you reappeared.

The bus driver would roar the accelerator, On and Off
a column of black smoke rushing out
and when he blew the horn
my eyes searched from one face to the other
until I would see you
running with a packet of biscuits in one hand
and a bottle of water in the other.

On the way uphill, I would puke,
you would wipe my mouth with your handkerchief,
give me water and an avomine.
I would rest on your shoulder and sleep.

Thirty years have passed by.
I am going to the hills of Darjeeling again.
I sit by the window
a stranger rests next to me.
The wind moans through the glass chink.

At Kurseong, the bus slows down to a low throttle
beside the same train station.
It hisses and comes to a halt. I do not want to go out.
And it feels like nothing has changed;
the same languid rush, the smell of coal and the faces of the people.

The driver comes back, pushes the accelerator, and blows the horn.
I look at the crowd. The mist curls up and lazily covers the town.

A COTTAGE BY THE SEA

Whenever I pass through places like Joneshaven,
with its fishing boats and their salt-bitten roofs,
I think about retiring by the sea –
an old, whitewashed cottage,
not too close, just near enough
to hear the tides each morning.

I'd like the locals as I pass,
to maybe say, 'There goes the writer,'
as I walk to the post office
with a loaf under one arm,
and a letter in my coat pocket.

The mornings would be soft with mist,
the sea spilling over the moss-covered rocks
like it's been trying for years
to smooth the sharpness out of things.

Further uphill, where the sea's sound does not reach
the old hills have caves
open like a mystery.
No one has been inside,
the silence within remains undisturbed,
centuries-old, like the rocks that surround it.

But I haven't done anything yet
to buy a cottage by the sea
and if you want to know where I am now,
pass the A90 in Granite City, Aberdeen –
you will find me there at Rosehill Avenue
still weaving my dreams.

BODY

My body lies in the living room.
All my family members have come
from Assam, Nepal and America
and those who could not come
saw me on their mobile phone screen.

This is the same room
where I have had hundreds of cups of tea
ate lunch, with you all.
But now, on this December night
there is tiredness in your eyes
but you do not want to sleep.

The house dog is quiet
in the coconut groves nearby.

The kettle boils tea for the visitors,
some step out the gate
to smoke a cigarette in between.
The night passes but not for me.

My body, suddenly a leaking burden
to be rid of at the cool edge of dawn.

IS THAT YOU

The night you died, father, the moon was beautiful
the best of the season, perhaps.
Blue, with a soft amber ring
as if the sky had lit a candle
for your leaving.

I held you close when there was still
some warmth left in your body.
I kissed your forehead and gently felt your lips sealed tight
as though some last words would slip out of them.

And when they lit the fire,
I watched how your body gave itself
to smoke, to sky
first black, then ash-grey
then a pale blue rising
spread all over the hills of Devghat.

You were perhaps in a hurry then
and no sooner the boats of the fishermen returned
there was nothing left of you.

Thirty years have passed.
Still, sometimes I walk at dusk
looking up through the branches
upward to the sky.

On a clear day, I often see that one, steady star
hanging above the world's noise,
and though I know
how far light travels

how long it lingers
still, I find myself asking,
quietly, without hope or answer:

Is that you?

LIFE

I often wonder where the soul goes?
Does it disappear into eternity?
Or does it mingle with the wind and become the fragrance of flowers?
Maybe it follows the river's long forgetting
becomes the silence inside the rain
or takes shape in the wind's quiet turning
across an open field.
Last year,
when my cousin died at twenty-four,
his mother wept in the courtyard,
her hands pressed flat against her chest.
'Where has my son gone?' she asked.
'When will he come back?'
I didn't know what to say,
so I told her this:
His soul has become a bird's breath.
It rises when they rise,
rests when they rest.
And when the bird's time ends,
the breath goes on
into another set of wings
another sky.
The life stays.
Quiet, unbroken.
Moving from shadow to light
the way morning finds its way
through the leaves.
So next time you see a bird
perched on a wire at dusk
or gliding low across the rice fields

pause for a moment.
It carries someone you loved
not gone, only changed.
Perhaps they are in the wind now
in the warmth of your morning tea
in the small pause before rain touches the earth.
And when you miss them,
close your eyes.
Breathe in, and say
'You are here. You have always been here.'

CAMPING IN CRAIGNURE

When evening trickled inside my tent
the sun had already turned into an orange flame
perishing behind the slopes of Craignure.
I poured some kerosene onto the coal and made a fire.
Blue flames leaped into the black haze of nightfall.
Near the camp, I lit a candle and covered it
with a slender open glass.

On the other side of the hill, the lake opened
like a mirror, unveiled after a vigil.

At midnight, I woke up to a sound and thought I heard
your voice. I lit the hurricane lamp and stepped outside.
The darkness and the lake had become inseparable.
Just the sound of water lapping gently on the rocks
and the wind in the trees.

A HUNDRED THINGS TO DO

I could have cleaned my Vauxhall Zafira;
seagulls have shit all over the roof
and grit as big as my fingernail
shines on the foot mat.

I could have gone to Raj da's house
and pressed my finger on a steaming glass of coffee,
watched the steam cloud over my spectacles.
I could have run along the hills of Bennachie
and stopped by the stream I found, to listen to the sound of water.
I could have placed my son on my belly
and sung him a nursery rhyme.
I could have even written a letter to my old friend
back in the hills of Darjeeling.
This June morning, I am just lying out in my garden
at the back of my semi-detached house,
hearing the lawn mower of my neighbour,
smelling the freshly cut grass that reminds me
of one hundred things I could have done.

WHEN I GO TO NEPAL

When I go to Nepal
I want to take a deep breath facing the north
and feel the mountain full inside my lungs.
It has been quite a while,
the longing has been pumped into my blood.
I want to go trekking this time.
I want to wake up at an unnamed lodge
on the foothill of a remote village,
hearing the sound of home-grown chickens
and the snort of pigs next to my window.
I want to drink tea from a glass smelling of kerosene,
take a bath in water boiled on a coal fire.
I want to get lost for hours and hours on the ridges
that live hearing the sound of crystal rivers.
This time I am not taking my laptop or my phone.
I have told my wife to pass along a note to all my friends –
he has gone to the mountains.

LOVE

The old mahogany chair sits near the window
as you left it; its hand-rest still hollowed
with the weight of your elbow. And as the evening wind
pushes little clouds of mist into our garden,
a heaviness stays. I remember those occasions
when we did not speak; sometimes for a whole day
and then another. Slowly longings would build up,
a strange desperation pressing on every inch of my body.
And then, we would speak up again, such heavy words
would queue at the back of my tongue.

It's been just two days since you left. My heart squirms
each moment I think of you. In the evening,
your blue nightie hung on the clothesline sways gently
as the wind fills up the hollow you have left forever. It swells
afloat, rises and falls back again, straightening its lacy folds.

Today, I have left the doors and the windows open.
Come home tonight and touch me.
Just like this wind that touches everything.

GRANDFATHER

Grandfather, I look at your portrait today,
at your white coat browned with dust.
Years of hardness lurking on the folds of skin
gathering on your forehead.
On the clear spring day you died,
the bougainvillea had climbed up
right next to my window
with its bright pink flowers, its roots spread
on the porch grasping every inch of earth it could hold.
It's already twenty years since you left.
I have married and divorced. I have two sons.
But it is your name I carry, like a medallion.
Next to your portrait hangs a painting on a nail:
a moonlit night, a swan is swimming on a still lake.
It must have been autumn then
the dark shadows beside the trees
must mean an evening somewhere and the phosphorescent light
must be the light coming in from an open field.
Perhaps an evening in Chitwan,
where the sun stays on the hills until late.
On a dry summer night the moonlight reaches
as far as the Mahabharat hills.
When the paddies ripen
wild elephants cross the river and graze in the fields all night;
the villagers bring out last year's firecrackers,
and when that fails
beat on tins and drums to scare them away.

THE SNOW

The snow is terrible this year.
The road towards the library takes longer than usual.
I keep the books home,
waiting for the roads to clear up.
Buses drag by
with chains on their wheels,
leaving long monotonous marks.
Smell of raw pines and chimney smoke
brings your memory back
in the thin December air.
The train shrills past every day
slicing the air between the hill and my house.

Your memory touches like wind,
and halts, at that moment when you left;
like one of those winter evenings.
The snow has been terrible this year.
The days longer without you.
Next year, I will wait
when they clear the snow.
I will watch from the hilltop
when your train comes
slowly, waltzing and whistling,
from the bends of summer.

MY FATHER'S DREAM

In the village where I was born
the sun came like a curse.
The land dried into fine powder.
The wind blew the dust like clouds.
My father worked like an ant.
He said, 'Earth is our mother.'
I have seen him grow potatoes, carrots,
millet, maize and yam.
The land in my village was a miser.
It took more and gave less.

Once during the marriage season
the harvest failed.
The field dried like a parched throat.
Fissures opened up like wounds in skin.
Frogs tanned to their small, dry deaths.
People folded like monks and prayed.
My elder sister had to stay home.
The man of her dreams never came
on a lean white horse.
Mother melted like wax in the summer heat.
Father shrunk like a scarecrow,
scratching the hard, baked soil.
All season, it never rained.
One evening, my father went to the wood
and never returned.

DAISIES

Towards evening, the sky darkens.
The yellow daffodils near my flat have
withered. The stalks droop low
each carrying its own carcass of petals.

Soon the daisies will push through the earth,
little by little, and will fill the meadow
long after the daffodils are gone.

By October, they will disappear too
leaving my head full of brightly lit flowers.

NEW YEAR

I just got up.
The half read book of Murakami's *Norwegian Wood*
pressed under my pillow. Its pages smell of pine.
On the desk, a row of books sit against the wall.
A burnt candle, pen stand and a book marker from Oxford
bathe in the dim yellow light of the table lamp.
Near my bed, the halogen heater lies under a pile of dust.
It will be winter again before I take it out.
My Facebook page has been filled with new year wishes.
Outside my window, thick fog has covered the town.
Raindrops splash on the glass pane and fall.
At the other side of the flat, my neighbour's TV is loud.
He does not know it is my new year.
I remember, as a boy, rolling on the sand of Rapti,
all night, like crocodiles.
We sailed on the wooden boat
in the pale blue light of the moon, like ghosts.
The other side of the river was pitch dark.
Even the shadows were chased out.
It was like another country, another time.
Shrieking sound of cicadas, echoed from the dense wood.
We never crossed the river.
On this side of Rapti, we made bonfires,
we drank all night, sang old Hindi numbers.
12, 1, 2, 3 – it was timeless.
The darkness gave way to a new day. A new year.
We woke up on the sand bed.
Hearing the sound of waves, Bote Dai singing far away.
Every year, when the new year comes,
the memory of the fire that night
keeps me warm.

DARJEELING

It was early February, a winter morning.
On an empty platform, the blue train engine arrived.
It coughed and belched. It hissed a jet of pure white steam.
I saw a blue hoarding – Darjeeling, 0 Mile.
Nobody filled or emptied the station.
Up on the ceiling, behind the mesh of iron
supporting the platform, the pigeons
had built houses. I sat until late, listening to their sound.
And then the train moved;
the pines, the loops, smell of coal,
the cold wind, the sting of winter on my skin –
and that bygone age.
Everything reminds me of Darjeeling.

THE ROAD TO ANNAPURNA

It was the second week of July.
The rain hadn't stopped for three days.
It fell over the hills
like a million crystal pellets.
Below the Annapurna range, clouds broke.
Streaks of lightning flashed across the lead-grey sky.
Rainwater poured over roof-tops
as houses silently gave up, letting the water in
through their weakest spots.
The red earth caked with fissures
holding slimy water, as a wound would hold pus.
The mud-filled road to Annapurna swelled up
like a wild python.
The wheel of my bike was caught in the bog.
It stood erect. Six men had to pull it out
with a coarse coconut rope.

At Bhoteodar, the sun dipped behind the hill.
We spent the evening, sitting near
the hearth at Kajiman's hut.
At nightfall, we shared stories
under the light of a kerosene lamp.
The shadow of the flame stirred on the mud walls
as the wind rushed in from the mountains.
We fell asleep listening to the sound of the river
and dreaming of the fish we had eaten that night.
Next morning, the sky cleared.
A jeep with the engine of a tractor
arrived from nowhere.
People squeezed inside it like chickens.
It seemed as if a whole village had got inside
to go to Annapurna.

MEMORY

No one tells me the name of my village
or the way that leads to my home.
A few years ago a bus used to go upcountry;
people rushed inside smelling of diesel and dirt,
of men, women, goods, chickens in coops and goats' farts,
sweat and tobacco.
The bus took everything.
The war has changed lives now.
They have burned the bus.
Children have given up school
and the past lives on only in pictures,
in the memories of the people
made silent by the burden of it.
The door of my home now opens to broken windows,
a shelled roof, silent bullet marks on the walls.
Wild flowers have forced their way in
through crumbled walls;
my childhood spreads here and there
all about the house.
The long afternoons are spent
collecting one by one
all that was lost
in the name of home.

FATHER

I cannot forget the day you decided
the morning wasn't worth waking up to anymore.

At the cancer ward, Bharatpur hospital
vials of medicines that failed you sat next to your bed.

The tubes were gliding out of your mouth like tentacles.
Whenever the white curtain at the door ballooned
the wind brought in the smell of Dettol-washed floors.
I was convinced you were asleep.
Outside, that February day went long.
The smell of wet earth after a light winter rain.
The green lawn splendid in the sun and in the middle
your body swaddled in white.

Your face shrivelled, somehow bluer than the sky that day.
There was a faint smile frozen on its way to your eyes.

That morning was the last time you held me.
I've forgotten what you were telling me then.

Twenty-five years have passed since that day;
sometimes when I am alone
I turn within myself for an answer, like you.

When all the noise settles down
I feel the weight of your hands
heavy on my shoulder.

THE BALLOONWALLAH

I remember the old man
who used to sell balloons when we were small.
He had a spiked bamboo stick
with colourful balloons festooned all over it;
red, blue, orange and white.
The man put mustard seeds inside it.
It rattled while we played.
He blew it till his moustache quivered
and the lines on his forehead straightened.
Sweat beads gathered at the tip of his nose.
He tied a drawstring at the end
and displayed it for sale.
He wore no slippers and smelt like fish.
He had long, calloused feet.
He entered the village with a small drum.
Later, the balloonwallah came on a bicycle.
Its tires crackled on a gravel road, raising dust
while we ran behind, our half-naked bodies
tanned mahogany by the August sun.
Our clothes fluttered along as we raced,
tearing the wind.
He had an iron canister fitted to it.
We bought the balloons, attached a letter
or sometimes a small message
and left it to fly on its own.
I wrote many letters
to my father who died in the civil war.
The ballonwallah used to tell me – pointing towards the sky –
the dead lived there
in the form of stars.
The balloons wafted up

till they could be seen no more,
even as we kept our eyes fixed on them.

CROSSING THE BORDER

We wait for the wind to push the clouds
to our side, just enough
to hide the moon this November night.
The air is sharp.
By now, the village where we stayed
has dwindled in the distance.
The warmth of the fire we made last night
still clings to our skin; faces we met
sink in our memory.
We push ourselves through the sugarcane field.
The sound of our feet
drowns the sound of leaves.
Leaves beating upon more leaves
as the whole field waltzes in the wind.
Dogs bark at a distance.
The air around us freezes.
Fear creeps, our breath is held low.
We leave our land, step by step,
walk through the night
towards the edge of the border
where our country ends.

HARVEST

It is only September and the fields have turned gold.
Soon the harvest season will come
when the paddies grow tall enough
to whistle with the wind.
The sparrows will come
and build nests on the roofs of houses.
They will weave strings of hay,
preen each other with their beaks
lay their eggs and wait 'til
all the nestlings fly.
People will build larders to store the grain.
Smell of cow dung and bamboo will stay
in the house for many days
until it becomes a strong memory.
My mother will wake up early
and cook food for the harvesters
who will come every day
with bandanas tied on their foreheads
and sickles on their backs.
During the day, scarecrows will guard our field.
At night, Father will stay awake on the machan
scaring the elephants with firecrackers.

THE NIGHT BUS

As I sit in my study stuck with a half-written poem
Jony the carpenter is humming a song. It's unclear
except for the You that stands out above the crooning.
It reminds me of a song I once heard on a night bus
to Kakarbhitta. An April night, a half-moon
hewn clear in a cloudless sky – almost like a lantern.
The gangway was stuffed with sacks of rice
and people with sleepy eyes. I had a window view –
the tinted glass pane opened wide. And as the bus
moved forward into the night, I rested my head
on the back of the seat, felt the wind lift the roots of my hair,
listened to the song and watched the moon
follow our bus all night.

THE FIRST SNOW

Anil, the winter that year –
the tarmac outside the *Gufa* Bar was slick with rain;
tourists rushed inside, plastic bags over their heads,
water droplets trickling down their wet trousers.
You sat near the fireplace, your back against the hearth
while the dry pine logs sputtered and hissed.
Flakes of ash flew off and fell on our heads.
The smell of coal came in from the train station
beneath the lower bazaar, its smoke hard to distinguish
in the grey fog heavy above the sky of Shimla.
I took a deep breath and felt the smoke tighten my lungs.
We drank Old Monk, mixing it with hot water.
As the night grew, a few boots clopped on the road outside
and then silence again, even the stray dogs were quietened.
The bartender closed the counter and sat down to drink with us.
The bell at the cathedral near *Ritz* rang twice,
and from the window we saw the snow
falling softly all over Shimla.

DEATH

In the first week of August, we moved to a new place
leaving that house where I was born. The garden,
the kitchen, the living room and the mango tree
next to my window where each season, nothing grew.
That year, the villagers were dying one by one.
The epidemic hit every house
killing everyone, almost as a god would –
I remember how my grandmother died one morning
letting out her breath in small installments
as though she was paying her debts to the life she owed.
Later that year, strangely enough, the branches
of the mango tree grew heavy with fruit.
From green they turned pink and yellow.
All over Bhojad, the streets smelt of them. At night,
the wind carried the fragrance as far as Devghat.

LATE SNOWFALL

That year, the winter came late.
The hills above Bennachie darkened before six.
The evenings wore the colour of dull smoke.
Yellow rapeseed flowers,
all over the field near our house,
shook in spasms.

The snow fell like shreds of fresh cotton.
At first, softly on the ground.
By night, the snow had piled, too heavy to melt.
We sat inside near the fire burning fir twigs
in the hearth of our living room. It sizzled,
crackled as the fire loosened the hardness,
turning the wood into coal and then ash.
We stayed late into the night
listening to the sound of the snow.

THE WATER MILL

At Tistung, the road bends behind a row of hills.
The narrow iron bridge creaks,
stretching its rusty hinges,
and lets through one vehicle at a time.
An old mill sits beside the stream, its roof
covered with green moss.
The mountain water rushes inside
turning the iron shaft, moving the grinding stone.
Towards evening, the air swells with mist.
Trucks carrying potatoes from Palung wheel back
with dipped fog lights shooting a tunnel through the haze.
Up on the hilltop, the children wait in the wind
for their parents, who struggle uphill
carrying sacks of millet for a long winter.

ONE EVENING

In the evening, the electricity fails.
The swami tree out in the courtyard rattles.
I light a candle and place it on the windowsill
as fresh swirls of raindrops slash on the window pane.
The wind brings the smell of wet leaves.
Thirty years ago, on a summer evening,
rowing with my dad across the Rapti
on a wooden boat, I heard a shriek, a female voice
coming from the wood at the other side of the river.
I turned around. In between the sound, the oars splashed
cutting ripples on the skin of water,
sound of water falling back into water.
It might have been the sound of trees
or something I never knew.
Today, in the rain, the soft sound of those oars
return to my ears,
and that shriek, as I sit beside the window ledge
late into the night.

REMEMBERING A LOVER

Now that my children have flown
to the far East, as far as Burma,
I have become an old man.
With each episode of numbness my body feels,
I know my bones are retiring.
I want to spend a few days with you
sharing how we could not live together.
How you had to marry a guy
who threatened to die
if you did not become his wife.
'He had even cut his wrist,' you wrote.

Then you had children; a beautiful boy and a girl.
And now forty years have passed
but my soul still seeks you.
Each day, memories travel
to the tip of my old mind and freeze.

I want to go back past your marriage;
past the long corridors of the college,
the boring lectures on Marxism.
I don't want to go as far as your school days.
I want to stop somewhere
around the first year of the college,
the year 1961, the month of December.
A sunny morning beside the long bridge
that linked your village with mine.

Your slithering black hair, falling
and rising like waves on your shoulder
as you walked towards me.

I touched you where?
First on your hand, then your face
and then emboldened, I reached as far as your lips
and kissed you for the first time.
I want to stop there forever.

EMPTINESS

There is emptiness, my uncle says
in the house where he lives.
It grows in darkness, feeding on silence.
Dreams of strange places
come home every night.
Not only the house,
the room where he sleeps
breathes loneliness.
The window looks to an open field
like a solitary monk.
And then the heart: a whole train of memories
looking out of the rusty window grills,
left behind on a ghost station.
It is all there, right there
where it aches the most.

MALEKHU

The fish are dried in the sun
skewered to their bones with a bamboo stick.
The stiff bend of their bodies almost poised as if to swim,
but there is no more swimming in the river now
after the fisherman's net, the hard kiss of death
on the head, the slithering and twisting on the mud.
The last dance before the dying
and the flesh crucified.
Nearby, a woman is heating mustard oil
on a black weathered frying pan,
almost ready to put the fish inside
for their last swim.

**Malekhu is a name of a place in Nepal on the way to Kathmandu, which is famous for fish.*

FIRE

Grey dust covers the city like a shroud.
Leaves roll like wheels, driven by the wind
that moans at my window, closed for winter.
Days fold, like a lacework of memories.
Each layer touches like skin.

You have been buried
for almost a month
at the edge of the churchyard
where the town ends.
The earth must be cold there.
The names of the body parts
you knew so well in school:
heart, lungs, kidneys and breast,
must have liberated themselves by now
inch by inch,
just as little by little you must have given up.

On evenings, when the wind forces
from our side door, I remember you.
I wait for you in the living room
beside the fire
while every bone in your body seeks warmth
deep below the ground.

MORNING DRIVE

Driving in the quiet hours of the morning,
the mist on my window, untouched,
the air outside moistened by rain.
Vapours rising like a million unseen wings.
Houses appear like strangers
at places where the road bends.
I open the window, the cold stings.
The air smells of wood smoke.
The forest down the lane is quiet.
Absence between one car and the other,
long and well defined.
Her face keeps returning like a force,
filling me with urges and sadness.
Last year when she left,
the same longing filled my heart.
I remember how, little by little,
I gathered myself.
I wait for the small moment
that happens in the passing
of people, places and things.

MY FATHER'S HOUSE

My father left a big house for me when he died.
The vault accommodated enough to let the space linger
between the earth and the sky.
A long concrete chimney rose out of the roof.
Father loved to see the smoke rise out of it.
He said it reminded him of something
he had to be happy about.

Evenings, he would sit in the loft
in a laid-back armchair, which he said was the only luxury
he could ask the world for.
He sat down till the sun went red on his windowpane
and the wood in the valley turned to faint mandarin sketches
on the horizon.

There is a room in the house where my father used to sleep.
Nobody lives in this room anymore.
The books are thrown all over the floor.
My father spent three decades in this house, this room.

After all the excitement of life, he now remains still and silent,
inside the photo frame
hung on the wall of this room, still smiling.
It was a pose he had taken, on my birthday:
well oiled moustache, hair parted in the middle,
a black mark on his forehead, to ward off evil.

There is a typewriter at the study table,
in one corner of the room.
It's a Remington 1946. Most of the keys are stubborn with rust.
An *A* would look like a *P* and if you were to type luck,

it typed a blurred and indistinct *uck;
the letters rode, one over the other.
Father had written hundreds of letters from this typewriter.

Near the window, there is a cage, where his parrot used to live.
Father had taught him to say *hello* and *goodbye*
to those who entered and left the room.
He said many hellos and goodbyes in a day.
Father fed him green chillies to sharpen his tongue.
One day he opened the cage and let it go
and the parrot never returned.

There is a piano at the other corner.
A dark mahogany-coloured thing, made up of oak wood.
It was musical in my father's time,
but now it has lost its melody.
A bunch of silverfish live beneath its pedal.
The notes burp and belch.
I tried to throw things out of my father's room,
to replace them with something modern.
But each time I enter, I am humbled by memories.

There is a grandfather clock he had bought in an auction,
stilled at one point for years, thick with rust.
In the middle of the room, there is a fireplace.
A bulky iron hearth, where he had spent countless nights
thinking about those things that are unimportant now.

At the end of the room a door opens towards a forest.
I feel like opening my arms wide
and shouting at the highest pitch of my voice,
loosing myself into the wildernesses.

HASIMARA

The train stops for five minutes in Hasimara
and a dimly lit platform emerges from the darkness.
Other than the light from inside the train,
there is only the light of the gas lantern
that hangs out of the station guard's room.
The smell of tea leaves drifts in from the darkness.
A few minutes walk from the station
my house lies at the edge of a tea garden
but I am not going there today.
As the guard blows the whistle
long shadows of metal carriages
shift shapes in the phosphorescent light.
My childhood memories, just like the train
chug through the dark,
into the vast countryside of Bengal.

THE LETTER

Your letter has been folded and opened
a thousand times, as if each time I am looking
for a star, or moonshine, in that old, creased
landscape of your writing.

I imagine the touch of delicate, tender fingers
moving between the cracks of words.
Your letter breathes you back.
I feel for the wind you have lived
in between the curves and hollows of your writing.
The sharp folds of your letter have moistened,
like this November evening, the air
suspended within the mist.
Winter rain sparkles in the electric garden light.
Restless wind-driven shadows
of the leaves shake like my heart.
Something shifts within me, perhaps
a space that opens towards you.

DEATH OF AN OLD FRIEND

Surendra, you used to give me boiled eggs
with ground black salt, cupped in your palm.
And pieces of honeycomb drooling with honey.
And we played hide and seek in the maize bush
at the back of our hostel.
I would always find you
crouching behind a row of trembling leaves
or up on the branch of a Neem tree,
your breath taut behind your closed lips.
In the end, our teacher used to call us back.
Now, I hear that you have gone hiding again.
It's almost winter now.
The clouds will soon turn to snow and fall
over the hills and lakes. I am beginning to worry.
I give up, friend. Won't you show up now?

JULY EVENING

Late July, the rhododendrons wilt
on their branches. The air is dry
and the rain still far away.
Strange birds perch in our backyard,
their bright plumes shine, as if newly painted.
They will stay there all day,
foraging for tiny insects
we will never see.

Late evening, the moonlight fills the window.
Smell of raw pine drifts in from Lumphanan.
At this time of the year, an uncertainty creeps.
You are hopeful and hopeless at the same time,
looking up at the summer sky,
at how it wants to get filled up, again and again.

THE VILLAGE

The house is not there, only the orchard,
the old mango tree hacked down.
Metre-tall ferns overgrow the worn path.
By the stone wall the kitchen runs down
to where my mother brewed rice beer
in the long winters. The white stones sit like
bare teeth on a bed of red dust.

This is where the family gathered during evening meals,
and laughed 'til late night, 'til the cicadas went abuzz.
I remember the bend that led to Regmi's farm,
but cannot trace the path further,
its russet-coloured slope darkened by the shadow of nettles.
During Dashain the path was lit with yellow marigolds;
bees drunk with their nectar lived nearby.

My village and I have both become old now.
But, when we meet, there is something that draws me in.
Life perhaps that I can't find elsewhere.

NEIGHBOUR

Quietly
the evening settles down;
my window half open
faint moon beams
mix with the light of my room.
Down on the pavement
my neighbour walks silently
back from his work
opens the door of his flat and stealthily goes in
and switches on the light.
He closes the blind of his living room
dissolves himself
in the semi-transparent light
sits down at one corner
and writes something
I will never know.

I like to see him
walk every night
into his flat
shut the blind
and turn into a shadow.

THE PHOTOGRAPHER

He comes every year
with a curious pair of eyes and a camera
fascinated by the black and white
status of my country.
He takes photographs
of street children
half naked and hungry.

Whenever he comes
the children flock around
asking for money or food.
He buys them a packet of chocolate
and takes photos
of their dark hollow eyes
unkempt hair and rickety bodies.
He won a prize last year.

His photos do not change
but what changes are
the children in the photos.

He knows how to auction their story
and the pain in their eyes
because he knows that people will buy pain
and are ready to pay any price.

LOSS

If my third child had survived
he would be in a nursery now.
I remember that day.
The wind had blown
through the forest floor.
A mess of brown, yellow and green leaves
had piled up nearby.

My baby was born that night
in the scant light of a kerosene lamp.
While the flame moved with the wind
he was rushed out in a flood of blood
down on the ground of a makeshift camp.
No hospital, no crying for milk, nothing like that.
He was so small as I put him on my palm.
I could see two black dots
in the place where the eyes would have been
and a lump in the middle of his unformed groin.

I knew he was a boy.
He had no hands that I could hold
or a heart that I could hear beating.

WINTER MEMORY

This winter, unlike last year,
the land lay frozen
cold, deserted and bereaved
as if a death had occurred here
right next to my house.

I remembered you,
how last summer
we went for long walks,
watched how people threw balls and sticks,
how their dogs ran after to fetch them back,
how children fresh from the nurseries ran,
while their parents watched,
how we trod on the brown leaves
in the garden near your home,
how the silence
between one and the other step
could be so deeply felt,
how we sat down on the bench
kept at the other end of the park
and stayed for hours
watching our shadows.

And how we walked near the pond,
made paper boats, and played all evening.

FAREWELL

We tied his body in a sling between two green bamboo poles
and bundled his bedding, his coats, his underwear,
his shirts, trousers and the Wrangler jeans
he loved so much.
We lit a bunch of jasmine incense sticks and shoved their points
into the flesh of an orange near his feet.
We kept his Seiko 5 watch, green Ray Ban glasses, a gold ring
and an aluminium box, full of diaries.
And from the bedroom window, we threw
a bottle of Horlicks, half-eaten digestive biscuits
and a few pears.

We tore down the calendar from the wall of his room,
washed the floor with Dettol. We locked the door behind us
and followed the way that led to the edge of the river.

In the evening after the funeral,
we framed his photo and nailed it on the wall,
the empty room waiting to be filled again.

IN THE DARK

Sitting by the window, in Berlin
the yellow laburnum trees
brightly lit on the pavement
I think of home.

It is night in Nepal
and in my house, in the back yard
my mother has planted cucumber,
pumpkin, chilies, and maize.

They grow in the dark –
the cauliflower rises to the sky in a dull embrace.
The beans curl up the bamboo lattice,
a millimeter at a time.
By the time my neighbour's cock crows in the morning,
the colours from the fields
will have silently entered the roses.
The papaya sweetens.

So many things grow
in the night, in the absence.

ACKNOWLEDGEMENTS

This book would not have been possible without the unwavering support of my mother, Chameli Chhetri, and my wife, Rupa Chhetri. Your encouragement and belief in me have been the foundation of this journey. I am deeply grateful to my brother, Prabin Chhetri, and my extended family – Arpana Chhetri, Sulav Timilsina, and Pramila Timilsina – for their continuous support and love. I sincerely thank my daughter, Sanoja Chettri, for meticulously editing some of my poems and my son, Sharvin Chettri, for his constant presence and inspiration.

This book is dedicated to the memory of my late father, Amber Bahadur Chhetri, whose blessings I seek as I present this collection. My profound gratitude extends to my supervisor, Wayne Price from the University of Aberdeen, and my nephew, Rohan Chhetri, who dedicated their valuable time and insights to refining the manuscript.

I owe special thanks to Todd Swift, whose guidance in pruning the manuscript and selecting the cover design was invaluable. My deepest gratitude goes to The Black Spring Press for publishing this collection and bringing it to life.

Many of the poems in this collection have been recognized in journals and competitions. 'Home and Grandfather' received the Nosside Poetry Prize in 2011 and 2013. 'In the Dark' was commissioned by the Stanza Poetry Festival in 2020. Poems from this collection were featured at the Edinburgh Poetry Festival in 2017. 'Paper Boat' won second prize in the Vancouver Tagore Poetry Competition in 2018, and 'The First Snow' was shortlisted for *The Oxonian Poetry Review*. Other works were longlisted in the Flarestack Pamphlet Competition (UK) and the University of Canberra Vice-Chancellor Poetry Prize.

This collection was supported by grants and awards, including the St. Peter's Foundation Award (Oxford University) for its earlier stages and a grant from Creative Scotland for its completion. I am fortunate to have been a writer/poet-in-residence in Portugal, Switzerland, France, Spain, Italy, and Scotland, experiences that profoundly shaped this collection.

Nabin Kumar Chhetri
Aberdeen, Scotland, 2026

The author thanks the editors of the following publications where some of these poems first appeared: *Reunion: Dallas Review (USA), Mused Literary Review (USA), Wilderness House Review (USA), Gutter (UK), Ink Sweat and Tears (UK), Apple Valley Review (Canada), London Grip (UK), Toasted Cheese Literary Journal (USA), New Writing (Scotland), The Istanbul Review, Wayfarers (UK), Reverie (USA), The Lamp (Canada), Madder Than We Look – Write Minds Anthology (UK), Nosside(Italy), Fade (UK), Kyoto Journal (Japan), Ink Sweat and Tears (UK), Poetry Scotland (UK), Voices Israel, Irish Literary Review (Ireland), S.N. Review (USA), Forge Journal (UK), Wayfarers (UK), Shot Glass Journal (USA), Ricepaper Magazine (Canada), Penny Dreadful (USA), The Sun (India), Nosside Poetry Anthology 2010 (Italy), Quest (India), Spinny Babbler (Nepal), Mawaheb (Canada), Poetry Quarterly(China), Fade Poetry Journal (UK), Cynic magazine (USA), Tower Journal (USA), Poetic Justice – Amnesty International Anthology (Scotland), Featured Poet of the week in Poetry Super Highway (USA), Taj Mahal Review (India), Revival (Ireland), Reverie Poetry Journal (USA), Sixers Review (USA), The Essence (UK), The Kathmandu Post (Nepal), Red Ochre Lit Journal (USA), Nosside Poetry Anthology 2011 (Italy), Birds Eye Review (USA), The Dupage Valley Review, Benedictine University Press (USA) and Verse Wisconsin (USA), Fade Annual anthology (UK), The American Asthetic (USA), Himal Magazine (India) and Canon's Mouth Poetry Journal (UK).*

‘One Evening’, ‘Death of an Old Friend’ and ‘The Water Mill’ won *The Madder Than We Look 2015 Poetry Competition*.
‘In the Dark’ was Commissioned by Stanza, Scotland’s International Poetry Festival 2020.
‘Memory’ was awarded the Nosside International poetry Prize (Italy).